VICTORIAN
AND
EDWARDIAN
WALTHAM
FOREST

Photographs of the period
1846-1910

compiled by
W. G. S. Tonkin B.Sc.(Econ.)

© Walthamstow Antiquarian Society (Founded 1914)
Vestry House Museum, Vestry Road, London, E17 9NH
Monograph (New Series) No. 13
1973

Reprint 1974
Reprint 1975
Reprint 1976
Reprint 1979
Reprint 1982
Reprint 1984
Reprint 1988
Reprint 1992
Reprint 1995

ISBN 0 85480 022 0

Issued in connection with the Forest Festival 1973 and published in association with the London Borough of Waltham Forest Libraries and the Chingford Historical Society.

Cover picture: *Leytonstone High Road, c.1898, with a North Metropolitan horse tram and St. John's church in the background.*

Back cover: *Funeral advertisement, 1897.*

VICTORIAN & EDWARDIAN WALTHAM FOREST

From Rural into Urban

The London Borough of Waltham Forest was formed in 1965 from the municipal boroughs of Leyton, Walthamstow and Chingford which in turn had developed from the ancient parishes of the same names. A local history collection had been built up in each area and so the photographs in this booklet are from the Borough Archives at Leyton Reference Library and Walthamstow's Vestry House Museum, and from the archives of the Chingford Historical Society. They cover the period of great changes from about 1846 to 1910.

In Waltham Forest, these changes came about, not in the popular idea of the industrial revolution with factories and mean streets springing up everywhere, but gradually, with the great metropolis growing larger, and the farms, fields, large houses and small cottages being replaced by railways, shops, villas, and rows of terrace houses. So Waltham Forest became part of the urban sprawl of London, with the majority of householders working in London and travelling to and fro each day. The population figures show a tremendous increase in the period, though the main increase in Chingford did not occur until after World War I.

Year	Chingford	Leyton	Walthamstow
1851	963	3,901	4,959
1871	1,268	10,394	11,092
1911	8,184	124,735	124,580

This development meant that the local parish government of the three areas had to be altered, under various Acts of Parliament, to cope with the problems which the increase in residents brought to the area—housing, roads, poor relief, sewage, water and gas supply, transport, street lighting, education, and health. So Local Boards replaced the parish vestries, then Urban Districts were formed, and finally Municipal Boroughs.

In 1848, Leyton was described in White's **Directory of Essex** as a "large and handsome village, with many neat houses embowered in trees . . .". Leytonstone formed "a large and pleasant hamlet" on the north east side of the parish. Among the residents listed were 6 farmers, 2 nurserymen, 14 carpenters, 13 boot and shoemakers, and 4 wheelwrights. In the same directory, Walthamstow was "one of the largest and handsomest suburban villages near the metropolis". There were "many large villas, with tasteful pleasure grounds, mostly occupied by wealthy merchants and others who have their places of business in London". There were 15 farmers, 10 grocers, 9 carpenters, 17 boot and shoemakers, 5 blacksmiths, 3 booksellers, 2 confectioners, 7 horse and gig owners, 3 hairdressers, 3 milliners, and 9 tailors. At Chingford, however, there were 13 farmers, but only 2 wheelwrights, 3 blacksmiths, 3 shoemakers, a saddler, a harness maker, a builder, 2 grocers and a tailor. It was described as "an irregularly built but pleasing rural village".

In Thorne's **The Environs of London** (1876) Chingford was still called an agricultural parish and village, and even Walthamstow was referred to as a place with its "houses being in outlying hamlets . . ." and with "country on the forest side varied and sylvan". Leyton, despite its fields being "much encroached upon", still had many market gardens and nursery grounds where roots, flowers and potatoes were grown for Covent Garden Market. However, formerly it was the "residence of many great City merchants and other wealthy personages. These have mostly retreated farther from the capital".

The construction of the railways in 1840 along the Lea Valley, in 1856 to Loughton, and in 1870-73 to Chingford, gave an impetus to builders and land companies to buy large houses and build estates of small houses in the grounds. The Revd. Thomas Parry, Vicar of St. Mary's, Walthamstow, wrote in his parish magazine in 1882, " 'Out of town' is an expression which was often inaptly used to describe a temporary sojourn away from our 'village', but now, alas! it may be literally true. Streets of houses, felled trees, and roads in construction, sadly remind us that we are being rapidly absorbed into the great city".

In Walthamstow, the area on both sides of the branch railway line between St. James' Street and the old village centre round St. Mary's, was developed first. More development took place near Wood Street station, at Hale End Station (later called Highams Park), and near the second Chingford Station by the forest edge. The two High Roads in Leyton and Leytonstone were also developed, and then estates were constructed in the grounds of the large houses such as Phillebrook House, Wallwood House, and the Great House.

Horse tramways to link the new housing areas and the railways came in 1871-2 from Stratford along the Leytonstone High Road to Harrow Green, and in 1889 (after an abortive attempt six years earlier) along Lea Bridge Road to the Rising Sun. A horse bus service linked Hoe Street Station and Stratford at the same time, and in 1890 a horse tram line went along High Road, Leyton. Chingford did not have any street transport until the electric tram service was introduced to the Mount in 1905.

Industry was not important in Waltham Forest before World War I, though there were many small workshops scattered about the area and some isolated factories.

Any selection of photographs is bound to be limited by what is available, and it is therefore remarkable that we have such a variety of scenes. The ones more than a century old depict a way of life utterly different from today, but later photographs show scenes which can still be recognised.

The peculiar geographical situation of the three parishes placed them on a gentle slope running down from the forest on the east to the Lea marshes in the west, with the largest area of high ground in Chingford. The forest has therefore always been a convenient place of recreation and a barrier to building, while the marshes provided a break in the continuous urban spread of London. These factors helped to give Waltham Forest a character different from the other outer London suburbs. In these views then, we see how Leyton, Walthamstow and Chingford changed from countryside into suburbia, from a rural into an urban scene.

The advice and help of Miss M. L. Savell, Mr. A. J. Britton, Mr. A. D. Law, Miss S. D. Hanson, Mr. C. O. Harvey, and Mr. H. L. Carter in this project are gratefully acknowledged.

The oldest photograph. Leyton Green c.1846, looking towards what is now Bakers Arms, with Capworth Street on the left.

Farms

Pimp Hall Farm, Chingford. The 16th century dovecote (left) and 17th century barn (right) still remain.

A view about 1890 from what is now Castle Avenue looking north west towards Larks Wood. The Warboys estate was built in the 1930s in the fields beyond the railway.

Hagger Farm, Walthamstow, in 1861 at the junction of Wood Street (foreground) and Forest Road. Here the Radbourne family built up a milk delivery service. Note the new lamp post.

Haymaking at Bull's Farm, Billet Road (between Garnet Way and Swansland Gardens). The last farm in Walthamstow to be built upon, c.1930.

Moon's Farm, Billet Road, was demolished 1927. The site is covered by Monoux Grove and Douglas Avenue.

Milking in the open at Moon's Farm. This property belonged to George Monoux in the 16th century.

The present Sir George Monoux School was built on this cornfield in 1927. The field formed part of Chestnuts Farm on which the Town Hall, Baths, and Polytechnic are built.

Public Houses

The Bell, Leytonstone High Road, in 1866 before the present facade was built.

The White Swan, Wood Street, started in 1838. Here it is about 1880. It was rebuilt in 1887.

The Bull & Crown, Chingford, in the 1890s, the predecessor of the present building. With the adjacent store, it was known locally as the "Town Hall".

The Bell, Walthamstow, started in 1857. This is how it looked before being rebuilt in 1900.

The Rising Sun, Woodford New Road, c.1910. Started in 1846, it was the terminus of the Lea Bridge Road tram line until 1931, and a favourite spot for relaxation.

The Kings Head, Chingford, stood at the top of a country lane before 1914.

The Royal Forest Hotel, Chingford, built 1880, was damaged by fire in 1912. The Chingford Volunteer Fire Brigade is seen in action.

The Common Gate, Markhouse Road, when built 1887-8 for £1,900. A good example of the confident style of the period.

The second Green Man, Leytonstone, in 1902. The present inn was built on the stables site to the left. An earlier inn stood further to the right.

Houses

Red House, Hoe Street, at the junction with Grove Road before 1890. It was finally demolished in 1963. The trees on the left belong to The Chestnuts, and the wall on the right to the Court House (now the telephone exchange site).

The Chestnuts, Hoe Street, was built in 1743 and was a private residence until 1894. It became a trade school in 1919 and is now used by the N.E. London Polytechnic.

Barclays, or Knotts Green House, now the site of Livingstone Tower. Rebuilt c.1786-91, it was the home of Robert Barclay (the banker) 1821-53 and his son Joseph Gurney Barclay 1853-98.

Nearby in Leyton Green Road stood the White House. A 17th century building, it was replaced by the Council clinic and White house flats.

Suffolk House in 1897 stood on the north side of Capworth Street.

*Essex Hall was the last of a succession of buildings at **Higham Hill** which were the manor houses of Higham Benstede. Replaced in 1786 by **Highams** (Woodford High School), it was demolished in 1934.*

The garden front of The Great House, Leyton, which stood in the High Road opposite the cricket ground. Built c.1715 by Sir Fisher Tench, it was demolished c.1904.

Wallwood House, 1892, stood where Chadwick Road, Leyton, is now. Built by William Cotton c.1820, it grounds reached to Forest Glade.

The hall and dining room in 1887 of Phillebrook House, Leyton. It stood between Leyton Park and St. Mary's Roads. The Phillebrook still runs under Coronation Gardens.

Clay Hill House in 1865 was in Forest Road, Walthamstow, where Priory Garage is now. Built c.1710, demolished 1887.

Uplands, Blackhorse Lane, was built 1836-38. Occupied as a house until World War I, it was demolished 1954. A garage occupies the site.

Friday Hill House, Chingford, was built 1839 on the site of an earlier manor house. It was the home of the Boothby-Heathcotes until 1940, and is now a community centre.

Hawkwood House, Chingford, in 1910, was situated in the valley between Pole Hill and Yardley Hill. Built c.1850 it was extensively damaged by a flying bomb in 1944.

The Lodge, The Green, Chingford, c.1905. It was one of many large houses built in the area in the 1890s. It is now divided into two properties.

Churches

The ancient parish church of Chingford was abandoned when the new one was built on The Green. It became a ruin, but was restored in 1929 through the generosity of Miss L. Boothby-Heathcote.

The exterior and interior of the new parish church at Chingford by Lewis Vulliamy, 1844. The present east end by Sir Arthur Blomfield was added in 1903.

The Wesleyan Chapel at Chingford Hatch in 1906. Built 1862, it was demolished in 1949 when the parade of shops was built.

A Sunday School outing from North Chingford Congregational Church, Buxton Road, some time between 1893 and 1897.

Marsh Street Congregational Church, built 1871, was the third on the site. It stood opposite the Central Library and lasted until 1965. High Street (name changed 1882) was a road of houses and cottages long before it became a market street.

Wood Street Union Church, 1900. Its successor still stands on the site in Vallentin Road.

The ancient parish church of Walthamstow (St. Mary) c.1900. The building was entirely remodelled during the 19th century.

The interior of St. Mary's c.1850, with the pulpit as the dominant feature and high box pews.

St. John's, Chapel End, was the first daughter church of St. Mary's, Walthamstow. Built 1830, it was replaced by the present church in 1922.

The Revd. Wm. Wilson also had St. Peter's built in 1840. The building on the left is the National School.

St. James' (1842) was the third daughter church. It was replaced in 1903 by a larger building demolished 1962. A health clinic stands on the site.

St. Mary, Leyton, in 1901: the ancient parish church. The cupola came from The Great House.

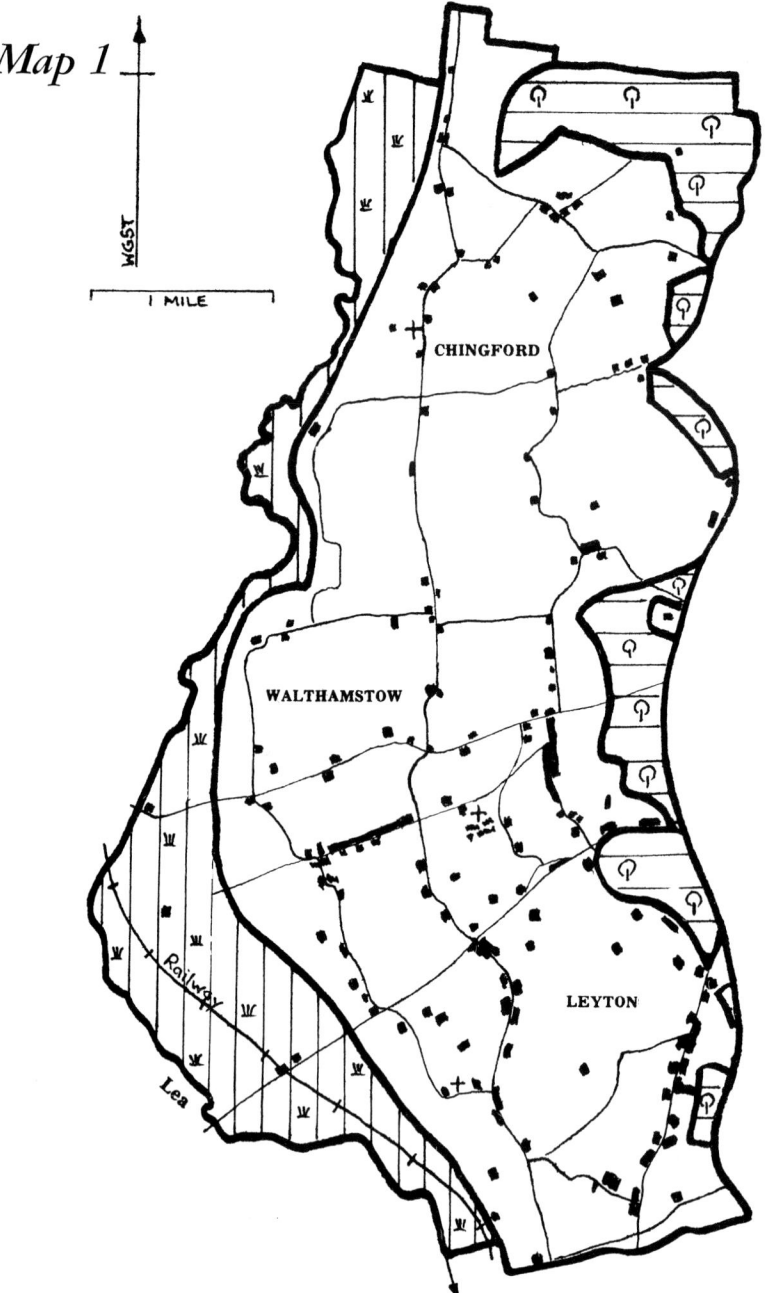

Waltham Forest in 1840.

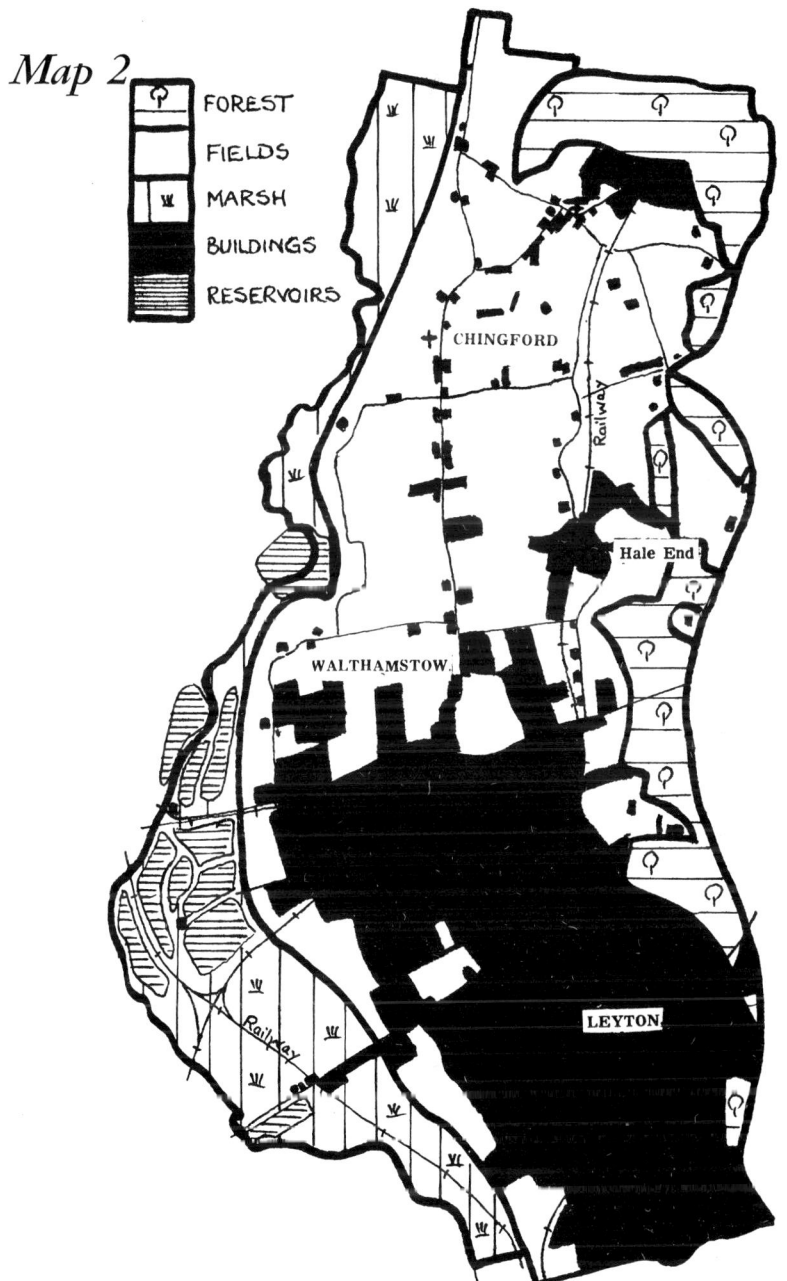

Waltham Forest in 1910.

St. John, Leytonstone (c.1898) was built 1832 to replace a chapel of ease. The building on the left was the Independent newspaper office.

The Mary Fletcher Memorial Church, High Road, Leyton, in 1897 on the corner of James Lane. Built 1877, it has been replaced by a petrol filling station.

River Lea

The Ferry Boat, Walthamstow, is an ancient inn which still stands. The narrow wooden bridge over the Lea was built in 1760 and remained until 1915. This photograph of 1853 is the second oldest in the collection.

Flanders Weir, Chingford, was on a branch of the Lea directly west of the Old Church. It was a favourite spot for fishing and swimming.

Transport

Hoe Street Station (Walthamstow Central) opened for traffic on 26 April 1870, but at that time was surrounded by fields.

Highams Park Station as rebuilt in 1900. The opening of the original station in 1873 led to the development of Hale End.

The first Chingford Station was opened in 1873 by Bulls Lane (Kings Road). Replaced in 1878 by the present station, it survived until 1953 as a goods depot.

This triumphal arch was erected at Chingford Station for Queen Victoria's visit to the Forest in 1882. Apparently it survived until 1909 when it almost fell down!

An early industry was the construction of horse trams at the North Metropolitan Works in Union Road, Leytonstone. The site is now the Co-op premises, Langthorne Road. This photograph c.1890 was taken outside the West Ham Union Workhouse, erected in 1840.

The River Lea flooded regularly until recent times. Here a horse tram in the 1890s passes along Lea Bridge Road towards Clapton near the water works.

Walthamstow Council opened an electric tram system in 1905, and Leyton Council did the same in 1906. Here track is laid at the Thatched House junction, Leytonstone.

An electric tram passes the famous Victoria Hall in Hoe Street, c.1910. The Hall was opened in 1887 and the Granada stands there now.

Chingford Mount tram terminus c.1910 as building development was beginning.

The new terrace houses and the tram line end together at Higham Hill (St. Andrew's Road), c.1908.

Roads

Leyton High Road in the 1870s. The public house on the left is the Coach & Horses.

Another view of the High Road in the 1870s, between Buckingham Road and the Coach & Horses.

Marsh Street (High Street) in 1860. 18th century houses between Hoe Street and Cleveland Park Road. The white house in the centre became the Conservative Club and the one to its left became the education offices.

Whipps Cross junction in 1861 looking towards the Forest with Wood Street on the left. Note the signpost in the tree.

A gate leading onto Markhouse Common in the 1860s.

Church Lane, Leytonstone, in 1876. The wall of the churchyard is on the right.

The post office in High Road, Leyton, in 1880 stood opposite the Three Blackbirds public house.

A view looking north c.1880 over Turner & Budd's stables, Wood Street. Forest Road runs from left to right. Fields stretch where now lies Fulbourne Road.

Budd's Alley lay off Wood Street near the Duke's Head. Demolished 1934.

Baker's Cottage, Blackhorse Lane, in 1895 stood where the junction with Goldsmith Road is now.

Oak Hill Cottages, next to the Royal Oak, Hale End, in 1910.

Church Hill, Walthamstow, in 1890 looking towards Hoe Street before the terrace houses were built. Rectory Manor lay on the right.

A horse tram entering Blue Row in High Road, Leyton, in 1897. Grange Park Road was built to the left and Blue Row was widened in 1900-01.

Benton's Shops in High Road, Leyton, were demolished 1905. Sedgwick Road is behind the tall building in the photograph.

Leytonstone High Road in 1898 with St. John's in the background.

Chapel End, Walthamstow, c.1900. The spire of St. John's Church in the centre. This is now Chingford Road.

Chingford Hatch level crossing seen from Larkshall Road c.1885.

Chingford Mount c.1910. Dangerous for cyclists.

Victorian terrace houses in Cassiobury Road, Walthamstow, built 1889 with downstairs bays.

Grove Road, Walthamstow, with two storey bays built in 1890s.

High Street, Walthamstow, in 1905 when the first motor bus service started. The Palace Theatre (left) opened 1903 and was demolished 1960.

Station Road, Chingford, c.1900.

Schools

The coach-house of Essex Hall, Higham Hill, was used as a private school and Benjamin Disraeli was a pupil 1817-21. Later the Cooper family used it for a very popular Sunday School.

Board Schools were built under the Act of 1876 to cope with the increasing numbers of children. A class at Maynard Road, Walthamstow, in 1880.

The Sir George Monoux School, founded in 1527, was re-constituted in 1886 and used this building in High Street from 1890 to 1927.

At Chingford, the National School in Kings Road started in 1856. Here is the staff in 1887 and the lady third from the left, Miss E. Prior, died in 1965, aged 94.

Sports Day in the street at Harrow Green Board School for the Queen's Jubilee celebrations in June 1897.

A class of girls at Church Road Board School, Leyton, c.1895.

The football team, c.1900, at Capworth Street Board School, Leyton.

The hall with classrooms leading off was the typical design for Board Schools. Newport Road, Leyton, 1904.

A Miscellany

The general election in 1895. Outside the Liberal Unionist Committee Rooms in Orford Road, Walthamstow, near Beulah Road. Edmund Byrne won.

Another early industry—the Xylonite works at Highams Park. The firm started in Homerton and transferred to Hale End Road in 1898.

Cycling Clubs were very popular at the turn of the century. This is Hainault Cycling Club, Leyton, c.1902.

Horse power was all important. Joseph Silk of Blackhorse Lane delivers coal in 1908.

Urban development meant increased fire risk, so the Local Boards organised fire brigades. The Walthamstow Volunteer Brigade in 1894 at High Street Fire Station (No. 116).

Leyton Volunteer Brigade had a steamer called "Surprise" which they won in a competition. Chingford Brigade's original station still stands in Kings Road/Pretoria Road.

Excavations by hand for Whipps Cross Lido in 1907 as a winter unemployment relief scheme.

Victorian Town Halls are expressions of municipal pride. Leyton Town Hall (1896) decorated for the Coronation of King Edward VII in 1902.

The Marsh Gate at the bottom of Kings Head Hill, Chingford, in the 1900s. Before the King George Reservoir was built in 1913, animals could be grazed on the common land there upon payment of dues.